Tis of Thee

Fanny Howe

a t e l o s

16

Ŧ Atelos

A Project of Hip's Road
Editors: Lyn Hejinian & Travis Ortiz
Cover Design: Ree Katrak
Illustrations and Graphic Design by Maceo Senna
Photography by Ben E. Watkins
Additional Production: Travis Ortiz

Tis of Thee

During the 19th century there were meetings between men and women of all races in America, meetings that changed the texture of the nation and its consciousness. These were sexual, passionate and secret encounters that continued from decade to decade without interruption. Most were violent and repulsive; some were casual and mildly nauseating; and a few were voluntary and truly intimate.

The children born out of many of these unions were often abandoned or absorbed into the larger society without true identity papers. Their particular brand of orphanhood had reverberations. For instance in the last decades of the 20th century, there was a kind of mass suicide among gangs of children in urban America that seemed like a collective outcry from generations whose past histories were interrupted. It seemed to arise from a repressed but visceral emotional history. (Without a past, can you imagine a future?)

Tis of Thee was written during that period in America. It concerns two separate, intimate, interracial love affairs that occur decades apart—one during Reconstruction and another during the nineteen-fifties. In the first part a white woman, living with her father in the town of Onset, Massachusetts, has a brief affair with a black fisherman who trawls for oysters. Their contact is brief but very intense and results in a pregnancy. She leaves town and gives the child up for adoption. A half century later, during the Cold War, a similar encounter takes place between a man in Boston and a woman who is excessively attached to her tyrannical father. Once again, she gets pregnant and her father makes sure the child is given away.

Their children were left to defend the ontologically absurd. During their lifetimes a racially mixed population both eroded and sustained a segregated society. Confusion about the source of a person's physical history affected every aspect of social life—legal, religious, educational—until color has become the American version of "a class problem".

The text was written first as a series of poems in voices. Later I realized that the language was straining for another sound. Fortunately I met Miles Anderson and Erica Sharp soon and they composed the music that is on the attached CD. With the help of Nya Patrinos, a set-designer and video artist, we found the three actors to speak the parts. They were Andre Canty, Paul Miles and Stephanie French. The piece was performed first in the Porter Troupe gallery in San Diego in 1997.

Acknowledgements:

Many thanks to Lyn Hejinian, Miles Anderson and Erica Sharp for their generous, inspiring lives and work.

Tis of Thee

By Fanny Howe

Characters:
  X: African American man
  Y: European American woman
  Z: Their grown son

Music by Miles Anderson
Directed by Nya Patrinos

Performers:
  X: Paul Miles
  Y: Stephanie French
  Z: Andre Canty
  Erica Sharp: 5-string electric violin
  Miles Anderson: trombone and electronics

Y:

In the days when I was still drawn to romance like gravity
calling an arrow to a bleeding target's red center
I experienced myself as a small child. Always waiting.
I lived with my father who taught me these facts—that people are
like animals who always herd with their own kind—that
the cost of cruelty in one life is the debt you pay in the next one
and that certain women have collaborated
in the failures of their times by remaining silent
and that these women only enter history
when they want to further their own cause.

His opinions terrorized me and drove me to the beach
to find another father. Miscegenation was still a crime. It was
illegal then that I should burrow my way through sleet and
hail to the grey doors of the oyster shed. I did it anyway.
I had always been disobedient.

X:

Falling in love was like having a slippery gray whale shoot
through her fingers. It made her remember her feet bleeding
from sharp shells curtained in mud; made her hard to be so happy with blood
linking her to the salt sea. Still like a boy in
trunks, her idea of a perfect day was to be alone in the mud, cut up by cracked
shells, with no one home up at the beach house, everyone gone.

It was always dusk.

No one was ever in the shed but us.
First time I brought her six oysters, I sat down with her and
shared hers. She swallowed three that I held up,
shell by shell, dripping, and then I sucked my three and gazed out at the melan-
choly cloudbank. So we sipped the seawater from the oysters and the slime
stood in for our first entry into each other.

Y:

At our very first encounter I knew I loved him
because I grieved when he went to the door to check the sky.
It was the only way.
One day I told him a silly little secret-that when I was a child, singing
"My Country Tis of Thee" I thought there was a secondary
and utopian country called Tis of Thee that belonged to me
and a few others. I imagined this country as a nation of outcasts—
outside history—like a series of unattached railroad cars occupied by derelicts.
He didn't laugh at me or the fantasy but instead he joined me in it
imagining that Tis of Thee existed between the two oceans
hovering above and pressed against
the boundaries of Actual America. And altruism was its only commandment.

X:

I told her that the citizens of Tis of Thee
would have no interest in power, and would squat
in secret, as we were doing, and their woodsmoke could veil them
from the whole prevailing society outside. Now we tried to believe
that a little veil of smoke could keep us safe.
I guess I was hoping she would feel easy enough
to trust me beyond that space in another higher one so I could feel safe too.

Y:

But later when I found out I was pregnant the fantasy left me.
I was terrified. I had to run away because
my father could tell when people were either pregnant or dying
long before they themselves knew it.

Now I have come to agree with my father—that much of humanity
avoids mixing with anyone but its own kind.
And how do I know that? Because my pregnancy
gave me the claustrophobic feeling of a person
who has lived more than once. I felt trapped in time.

But will I ever know what I did in an earlier life to deserve
the blows I earned in this one?
Was I a cruel mistress to slaves and their children?
Did I even love this man, whom I hardly knew, whom I was forbidden to know?

Who was he?

Z:

He was born in the south—both times—to parents who soon traveled north.

They passed him back and forth face up between them with a roughness that
was not unloving.
He stared into the passing trees and their leafy chaos became the emblem
of liberty and security for him. He neither pointed, nor cried out when
he was growing up. Instead he had the silence of one who is flying.
In fact he was really just thinking; he would always be lost in his thinking.

When Boston was still too big for him to navigate alone, he was taken to Franklin
Park zoo by his mother, and later his guardians, on a regular basis. They would
see the birdhouse, talk with a parrot, then stare at the monkeys. Those Sundays
were dominated by another model of the civilized world:
a circus.
There he saw a giant man with a lantern jaw seated in a clean suit
on a platform. He would never forget him.
If this giant had been an elephant, he realized, people would regard him
with affection rather than horror.

X:

I was born (again) about forty years into Reconstruction
following the unfinished Civil War.

Every time I heard the song "Old Black Joe" I remembered my mother
collapsing into a little caged creature. When she heard Hitler on the radio,
she would hand me a stick of gum. Its soft sugary and cold belt was like an
indoor slide.

My father had been blown to bits in North Africa. Soon she gave me away
telling me to trust nobody.

Z:

In those days the Hill viewed across the Charles River was like a little round kiln
with a gold dome on top.
One square foot of water was as beautiful as the whole of Vermont
viewed from the sky. When he walked on the grass in Franklin Park
his mother's hand never held his. She didn't want him to be dependent on any-
one. A lonesome boy he saluted at ballgames
when they played the National Anthem, then folded his arms across his chest
conscious of too much visibility in existence.

At The Home for Little Wanderers, an orphanage, this feeling grew in him.

He read philosophy and decided that phenomenology is the 20th c. equivalent
of the mystical notion of a mechanistic body.
The soul was an uncreated element straining for a life
in space. . . A disturbance in one's relationship to the face facing oneself
could set off a reaction of dread. . . . Few people can look directly at someone
who doesn't remind them of themselves—or of someone they know well.

He knew ways to analyse hierarchies since he was raised on the late l9th centu-
ry's Social Darwinism. He had read about the Little Mermaid and her ascent
through the gravities of heavy seawater to the angelic orders.
Later he would talk of undinism, piss spraying Hitler's face.
But he was able to analyse Undine among cherubs in the cloud formations, and
believed that humiliation was the link between the two meanings.

He longed to be like an American Indian rowing without making the slightest
splash. But he had to scuff through the leafy pavement instead, feeling his grief.

X:

One day I realized that all sounds and sights could be raised about a yard above the place where I sat and leave me free.

In my life before the Civil War I loved books. Many white people were edgy about letting me and my people learn how to read. Especially the Bible.
They hated us reading that.
But I would not be deterred and not only read it, but learned it by heart.

Y:

I only remember things in my sleep
where the insurmountable present forces me to be nostalgic.
However on a certain kind of dry day
in the city a horseshoe crab clatters through the tide
in my ear, batting at blackened oysters clamped shut among
the stones. It's 1890 again and the battlegrounds have not even
begun to be planted with new crops and housing.
I am wandering down to the beach to the stone jetty where the man
is cleaning off the oyster shells.
Are they more stone than bone? I ask him, and he shoots out a laugh in response.
I notice his long brown hands and the thinness of their bones.
He tells me his father and he came to Cape Cod
from Shiloh after the assassination of President Lincoln.
I am the educated only child of a solitary man and can easily
engage in political conversations, and do. We both agree,
there on the stone jetty, that it will be at least a hundred years
before the Civil War has been settled.
I remember this man as bearded, with the look of a Hindu
about his wide brow. Hardly any eyebrows made his wisdom shine.

Z:

They take to meeting regularly on the rocks, then she goes out in his boat
and his cart with him. How like looking through seawater
is the work of the memory. When she turns on her interior torch
and holds it toward a flat surface she realizes
that only the outlines of the past can be seen.
Yet it's the same past, twice!

Y:

Our little boy was conceived in the back seat
of a red carriage on a rainy night in Onset.
Rain steamed the interior.
The man laid me on the leather with the tender
solicitude of someone beginning an ending.
After that I haunted what I myself had done.
Like an erotomaniac who covers herself with the night
I was frightened of myself!
And so I ran around asleep with my hands on my cheeks
trying not to scream or speak for fear
of alienating my own body. And naturally I didn't dare
pursue him openly. Not in the eyes of this society.
Sometimes the past rises like a huge porpoise and tosses
that flat surface aside. Ox-blood red, and wounded.
Yes, my interior sometimes opens and closes like parts
of my body that work outside the will and I am aware that I am
living each day with a complete stranger who is myself!

X: (sings) Wade in the water. . . .wade in the water. . . . .)

I am, however, stamped throughout my cells
with the United States Service, as if a square root of my blood
were a postage stamp. I am sure that I have been poisoned
by the society I occupy.
Now the rich and the fortunate are one.
They used to be separate, did you notice? They said
it was better, then, to marry a lucky boy than a rich one. Now
they say it's one and the same thing, but I think they're wrong.

Z:

She gave away most everything she loved. Out a door and into the cosmetics
of city walls, she was as white as potato flour on a block. Nearly invisible.
She never wrote to tell the oysterman about the baby
because her love for him was weak in comparison with her fear of her father.
She always received her father's letters in hospitals and other homes
but didn't need to read them
to guess what was inside. Another lecture on female behavior
in regard to voting rights and birth control.

Y:

He would write: All right, my dear, let's talk about liberty in a really deep way.
Who owns women and children? What is the economy of the female body?

X:

I too cross-examined her, in my mind, after our three weeks together
beside the sea, and I decided that white women didn't know themselves.
The ones who collaborated with their men and backed them up in their acts
of violence found a way of maintaining power without having to take
responsibility for it.

Two generations later I would conclude that most women
are as close to being equal as clocks are, which made them more secure than
most men, and also that white women in particular were becoming
their own servants and slaves, as if wicked histories had returned to haunt and
possess them in their one lifetime.

I speculated that white women could form a natural and happy bridge
for the colored and the poor to escape their conditions.
Love and marriage could be the gentlest kind of revolution
where race and economics were leveled.
Yet violence was the preferred course of mankind.

Y:

Across one century, and into the next, I became the mother of his child—
Twice at least—but let each child be taken away from me.
Naturally I grew nauseous from loneliness.
By night-fits and shadow-language of the trees I tossed
my knees this way and that—my bed a raft on a sea ill-lighted and deep.
My cries were dry.
The leaves rattled the glass.
Outside sirens would invent the whole city's anthem,
a tune of anonymous personal pain,
and trash cans smashed against teenage hands. Now I would see
reflections like stains in a clear swamp. . . . White lilies cupped by greens.
Trees twinned and echoed on a glassy pond.
It was really a mirror for me. My birthright with its clear glass tables
in livingrooms—except where the cocktail left a circle—or the peanut a shower
of salt—was never to be mine again.
I had stepped outside a magic circle.
And I couldn't take care of myself
even though I could talk eloquently about many liberating subjects in 1890.
And yet again in the middle of the 20th century.

Z:

She knew that he knew her limits even before she did.
Often she crossed the Charles River on cold Saturdays
to watch the speakers in Boston Common;
they were old abolitionists and poets with questing and optimistic eyes.
After all, non-native Americans were never sacred people with leaders
who received their power as a birthright. So it was easy for them
to forget the incarnation and be grandiose instead.

The arrival of a Messiah is said to bring a flash of self-recognition,
but she was only looking for a normal mortal
to give her directions.

X:

After she left I worked the sea for oysters off the Cape Cod coast.
From my little dinghy I watched the faces of far-off whites
as they lifted and drooped over the sand, scooping for clams.
I wondered about them.
The moon is what is seen by the light of the sun.

So whiteness is what is dependent on a witness.
The moon's opaque and egg-like sheen is the kind of zero
that wants to be more than air and negativity.
This zero wants to be counted as one of the numbers.
Likewise the moon is a blank whole, instead of a black hole.
It makes us believe that the sky is as solid as whatever is in it.

When I returned to shore, and was luckily ignored, I looked at the sea grass arch-
ing away from the green wind and took it as a sign to move northwest.
Thanks to sight, we don't know where we are going.
Forms are confusing. Paths split, we make judgements.
People meet, hate or imitate, and reject, indifferent.
I knew this, but took an insane risk when I talked to a white woman intimately.
She came forward first, of course, as if offering her body bravely as a
sacrifice to history. And I believed that she, being white and privileged,
knew what she was doing.

She lay near me with her eyes closed, listening to stories from a world
so alien, they might have been legends.
Her passivity peaked as her rebellion weakened.
For a brief time, in such a state of abandonment,
the situation seemed harmless.

I didn't condescend to her, although it was the time when women did not have
the vote and should have been treated with justifiable contempt
given the fact that former slaves who had been denied education and training
in the running of the nation, were sent into a hostile society, and few of these
women, who should have been their allies, did anything to help them.
I knew I could be killed by one slip of her tongue to the wrong man.
And pregnancy was a guarantee of my being lynched.

Z:

It was, for people like him, a time of terrible trial.
After the end of slavery, the economy gained momentum like something freed
from the controls of law and ethics. Now greed increased like a lurching wheel
on a down curve. Mass cattle production, stink of skin, cow meat meted out to
feed the meat of the human intestine.
Measure for measure, money eliminated a concept of value based in physical
quality.

After the Civil War, the country was like a late summer farm.

The farm was preparing for market and people rushed by sucking,
sweeping, pushing, retreating, contracting, pulsing, eyeing, eyes as periscopes,
crystal balls and bubbles, myriad-made, implicit, insistent, variegated, spirit-
members managed, produced, distributed
and there was no attention or shelter for the weak, the chicks.
Owners were too busy wondering:
Who is longest? Who is fat? Who is cheapest?
Who is best? Who is measuring?
What's my credit? What's my debt?

Y:

And the weakest like me were aware of one fact:
My body is free of me. I know this because when I want to die, it doesn't; and
when I don't want to die, it does.
And this knowledge helped me both to survive, and to die.

Z:

How could a human woman abandon her child to such chaos?

Y:

The baby was taken from me at birth. December 15, 1890.
So the first time I didn't exactly abandon him. He disappeared.
My father came and made sure he was put in an appropriate place for a child
like that.
He would never tell me where. His control over worldly matters
would always evolve into silence.
I tried to believe it was for the best, when he disowned me.

Still, something was never right in me again. Like a dog
I followed postmen on their beats, sometimes getting letters I never read
because they weren't addressed to me.
And sometimes I followed shadows and sometimes heat.
The city steamed around my knees—winter's breath from sewer pockets,
while I shook like something held to the wind.
My father would not allow me to return home.
Strapped, then, into the tunnel of a century, I couldn't shake free
to airiness again. I had carried the baby long beyond term,
and still felt it kicking.
It made me wish for a second chance with the same man.
And that obsession took hold of me. . . .Walking and wishing
correspond. I kept at both experiencing time and space
as twin illusions I had to penetrate. No, dissipate.
I felt sorry for everyone. We all together
begged for rewards and returns. Nothing happened!
Nothing changed! I couldn't find the baby or the man,
no matter how anguished was my prayer.
I searched everywhere as in a naked nightmare
and saw more and more little boys growing around me
inch by inch past my knees and hips.
Their sweet red lips, soft brown skin, sticky fingers
and their dark almond eyes. What people called "their race"
could only belong to someone else. Not me. Not me. . . .

X:

Despite the dangers I tried to locate her when she ran away.
I tried to find clues in things she had said. Clues to her feelings, that is.
For instance, she told me that she was twenty five
before she discovered a way to end
her yearnings. And that time, outside the oyster shed and in the cart,
when she experienced the revolutionary sensation,
she couldn't believe it had been there, waiting, all that time,
and she hadn't known it. She said she hadn't guessed that—

Y:
—pleasure was the only way to murder
desire.

Z:

The truth is, fear slaved her, made her walk
in square cartoons where the cry "God!"
meant hesitation if not cowardice.

Through her two eyes an infinity
of materials that were invisible
to others would slide into her world
until she felt both owned and unleashed.
She knew she had broken the law and was outside it forever.

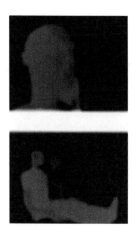

X and Y:

If you are guided by love, you are always outside the law!

If you are guided by love, you are always outside the law.
If you are guided by love—

Z:

—you are always outside the law!
That's how the century passed. In a day of lawlessness and excess.
And he? And she?
She died in a settlement house at the turn of the century.
And as for him, her disappearance aged him prematurely.
The silence of her departure was like a frost.
Embarrassed that he had actually hoped that she might lead him to a more
secure life he was finally just glad that he had survived the contact at all.

So given all his reading, bitterness and smart talk, in the next century
he entered the field of education and taught colored children. But in the Fifties,
because of his curiosity about Communism, he was fired, and worse.
He claimed that a loyalty oath, like a love promise, should be an affirmation
and not a list of denials.
So FBI men knocked on his door at night and came inside in heavy coats
and placed their walkie-talkies on the table.

They were after information about African American professionals,
Jewish lawyers, leftist ministers, but they got very little that was useful and left,
promising to return with the correct identity of the person they were after.
A negative identity, his, based always in what he refused to do.

X:

I wanted only to teach the ideas of Frederick Douglass, Emma Goldman,
and then the actions of Union and Civil Rights leaders.
In this country every progressive success is erased
by a generation of haters. Nothing can go forward!
On this score—and its awful consequences—I would never be silent
Why is the Left given criminal status
and its traditions erased from schoolbooks?
In the late fifties I left the city
where sirens played the whole city's anthem
a tune of anonymous personal pain
and trash cans smashed against teenage hands. Now I moved near the sea.

Y:

Here white lilies were cupped by greens
and trees twinned and echoed on glassy ponds.
Like a mirror for me. A birthright. A magic circle.

X:

And there I met a white woman who said she felt strangely drawn to me.
It was mutual. We sat on a stone jetty, talked and grew close.
She spoke of loneliness that was like a raft on a sea ill-lighted and deep.
So we hid away. And she tossed her knees this way and that
speaking a shadow language, both of us terrified we'd be caught.

After a few weeks she disappeared, and the longer she was gone,
the more I thought something terrible should happen to her.

Z:

But he was not a violent man as much as a violent thinker.

He became obsessed with one question.
Is social equality equivalent to the theological concept of mercy?

A priest said to him, "If you really take responsibility for the fact that you exist, you will find mercy everywhere."

But he understood the meaning of mercy less than the meaning of equality.

He longed only for the numbness of fishing in cold water,
even as he wandered the city brooding on the problem of equality.

Y:

I had learned a good deal just from sitting at my father's table.
But it was he, a schoolteacher,
who opened my eyes to the political realities
and their effect on all Americans.
That is, I began to know my own limitations.
While we sat side by side in the dark, gazing across the wrinkled water, he said:

X:

You have to face facts. Abolitionists preferred the idea of a free slave
to the actuality of a free man or woman.
Freed slaves have been given neither shelter nor training.
So the nation is like a market in full operation
resulting in ruin for those who have no training.

What is visible—animals first—and determined to be lacking an interior life—has
decided the nation's future course. The logic goes like this. If animals lack a
soul, then so do people who don't resemble the ruling class.
The proof? You will see. Civil rights and religious liberties will mirror
each other's progress through the courts.

X:and Z:

Any discussion about race is really a discussion about the creation of
the universe.

Y:

Now I believe that when the Messiah comes the world will have no images,
since the image will be cut free
from the object, released like beef from a cow,
and competition will automatically founder
as an instinct, having no visible object in sight.
Then on that day I won't have to look for you in order to know you.

X:

That's correct.
And what if you had asked me to leave with you, or you had written to me later?
I'm sure I wouldn't have responded, like you fearing multiple
and unpredictable consequences.
No one would want us around.
In such a world we might as well enter a circus, be freaks.
But I couldn't resist knowing if I had made a mark on you or not,
and found out where you planned to give birth.

But I misunderstood the situation.
While you were in fact assigned to a kind of hospital,
it was one that was called Mercy. A hideout for wayward women.

Because the place was in Boston I went across the paths
along the river there, just to look, holding my heart
that had already been assigned to an adoption agency once,
and I couldn't bear imagining my child's heart suffering the same fate.
But of course he did. Suffer it. His half-caste all lost heart, gone.
A male infant.
The groundskeeper told me about his birth and the nurse,
a nun,who took him away. To where? To what?
So, cowardly, I turned back instead of going to claim him as my own
and filled with a desire to break a law, and afraid of that too.

Instead I was cursing you with questions as I ran:

(Z: motherfucker, motherfucker, motherfucker. . . .)

Traditionally a motherfucker is someone—like a slave-holder, for instance—who forces mothers to have sex with him.
It is not, and never was, someone who fucks his own mother.
Did you know that?

Y:

All I know is I went through a kind of conversion
after leaving Mercy alone on October 13, 1955, 10 am.

That day a net of rain was cast over a church as if to capture secret believers
and draw them to the sky. I sought shelter on the steps then slipped inside,
remembering that it is better to enter a church for shelter from a storm
than for the consolation of its ikons.
I wanted to die.
I visited there a statue of St. Elizabeth of the Shadows.
Gems dotted the coal color of her frame.
Since I was often walking with the baby's ghost locked inside of me,
I could identify her blackness as the perfect environment for budding.
Assumptions were made by on-lookers:
You are a white one who is just like us?

No, I wanted to tell them,
I am a dark one budding from inside the skin.
Like St. Elizabeth.
I looked up at her face as if from the source
of a well, and knew salvation, or meaning, existed.
Stop, look and listen, they warned us as children.
I did so then. Once again I changed my mind.
Every attempt to complete myself through suicide
ended like this. I experienced my shape
as a loose garment made of signs and emblems
which would cover my cadaver through eternity.
But now I knew I must attempt to immerse my materials
in the waters of time. This would be the only way
to be streamlined. A free spirit.

Outside the church I pretended I was with my man
strolling in Tis of Thee and later in a schoolyard
where snow was lounging along boughs
making me wonder if I was the only one to see their beauty.
So many things are placed in so many places
and so many place themselves where they are,
I have to wonder what we are all supposed to see.

I suppose it is in some sense lucky
to be one of the undiscovered,
one of the hidden lost people.

When I am looking for something that I have lost, and I always am,
the objects around me become uncannily heavy and humid
as if they breathed and hid.
When I am, myself, lost I become uncannily heavy
and sweaty and breathe too high in my chest.

Lost from what?
I haven't even been found yet.

Z:

It is said that the Messiah will not come until the tears of Esau are exhausted.
Until Hagar's tears are wiped from her face and she is welcomed home,
there will be no peace.
That's the kind of language that this kind of man understands.
As a teen—sort of a prodigy—he became a public speaker in Boston Common,
talking to passersby on Sundays.
He lectured on race and history.

X:

Since the country was founded, there has been racial mixing by rape and by
choice, by marriage and by fornication, and it has acted as a kind of politics of
infiltration—a smear campaign against the homogeneous
but not quite enough to successfully achieve a national mixed identity.
Now, had there been more fooling around, sooner, the country
would be much stronger and happier.
Instead, American lawns green and shaved in the suburbs
call to mind the last stages of rhymed verse:

Y:

book leads to look
snow leads to blow
rose leads to grows

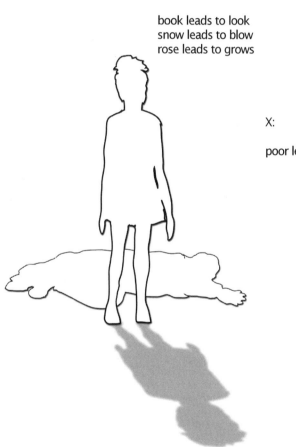

X:

poor leads to war

Y:

If "white" means that nothing has happened to a particular body
to disrupt its ancestral history;
if whiteness means extreme individualism, I was no longer white.
Instead I was something else—a secret American—secretly loyal to the father
of my errors, although he didn't know it.
I learned to renounce a sense of independence by degrees and finally
felt defeated by the times I lived in. Obedient to them.
Like someone on a winter day, among blocked cars, crumbling tunnels,
who shores up her energy with a spot of whiskey.
Minimal relief for surviving everything,
not a stirring up of the glands and hopes for the future.

I lived for a kind of escape, which I only found in the wonderful cover of night.

Sometimes alone at night I would reach the level of our conversations
by the sea as if they had a transformative radiance.
And this way I learned that knowing is "built in".
We are, sure enough, little cave-dwelling particles
of universe. I wish I could tell him this!

X:

If you live beside the sea and under the big sky
you feel a wonderful openness.
The shapes of the city destroy this sense of a given liberty.
You only find it in your dreams, or at night.

One night I directed my steps to the place where she stayed.
The semi-circular hill appended to the Catholic Convent was slippery
with accumulated leaves, paper and twigs.
The chilly bare branches seemed hilarious
among themselves like the laughter of boys on a field trip.

I breathed deeply, cooling off my innerverse, when I saw her passing
back and forth in front of the window. A mist shrouded the place
and made her features as soft as the glass on a lightbulb.
A yellow light burned within although the sun had risen.

I was tempted to tap on the glass, to go so close that I could see
her entire form as it glided back and forth
in the asylum. Was she pregnant? No, not again.
But I could taste and smell her from the shrubbery's damp enclosure.
I knew her.
For a flash I imagined taking her away to another country, a child between us.

Drenching under the branches,
I went up to the window and hesitated just before tapping.
Inside, rows of women in distress sat in nightgowns at a long table,
and when she screamed they all saw me and screamed too.
These shrieks were not warbles or sobs,
but high-pierced sirens, and I ran from them, with my hands on my ears.
Half of me was laughing.

Z:

Everyone American by a certain age has seen a blinking
red light multiplied in raindrops
on a windshield. How beautiful the way it kills
the pain of the accidental: redness illumined.
Tincture of iodine reddens and stings what it heals.

The police chased him into the trees. The solid reality of his dark
and foreign form terrified the woman.
After all he had told her that while religious issues
haunt the Constitution, few see the link between them
and biases based on appearances. Bank cards and windows
like grilles where Carmelites hide in their habits
make physical links invisible to the economy.
I mean enemy. Nobody voluntarily enters a force field
dominated by rage and the body.
Or do they?

She became hysterical.
The doctors shocked her electrically to find out what they had done together.

Y:

My father was right. In the end I hid my fraud and never DID anything.
I can't even blame the men for their power.
Whoever can, will.

X:

How do women justify their silence? Can they only say "my father was right"?
Seasons have come and gone, the snow dressing the wrought iron fencing
on Beacon Hill for decades, boats chattering over the cold oysters
in Boston Harbor all that time
and still the social structures have stayed almost completely the same.
Otherwise why did I end up in a holding cell?

Z:

She has no answer to this question, not really, but sometimes she claims that her persistent search for a way to live without being seen was a kind of prison too.

Y:

However, soon enough I discovered
that if you are alone too long, you no longer exist.
Except as a coward.
And if you never look in a mirror, you feel forever young
but hideous. If you are white
and have carried a baby who is not, that baby's body
becomes one with your own and you are darker and deeper for it.

Z:

Only you know that you are now a carrier of other histories, ones never
introduced before into your bloodline. Everyone outside
continues to see you as white all the way through,
but you are a new creation,
a completely unknown quantity, an equalizer
who can't be incorporated into the social body, a citizen
who is a witness to all sides of history.

Too bad you didn't take action.

X:

For my part
I can still pretend that the world is all right, when
I'm truly free. Alone, outside when firs and birches etch the snow like wood-
blocks
in the margins of a children's story.
My eyes recede to make room for my silence, and at these times
I prefer the visuals to any more speech.
A thorny black forest has a message
that can only be replicated
on film or in paint, though one longs to speak for them.

Z:

Have you stopped to look at the projects,
at snow on trash and brick?
On the horizon the city
is cut from stone cloth into the evening sky.
Rubble leads in all directions. Franklin Park
is hopping with starlings, the firstfruits
of a winter sky hang on trees.
From Humboldt Ave to Blue Hill Ave
Nubian notions are glued to store windows.
The children—social orphans—on stone-dented buses
have traveled the breadth of this city, joggling and pressing
at each other like mobs of unwanteds
who will only too soon struggle in a kind of mutual suicide pact.

Y:

I just hope that when I die I will see my lost children again.
And then we will drift off to Tis of Thee together.
In Tis of Thee we don't think memory is as powerful as moment itself.
We can solve playground fights because we see the world
as a nursery where spirits can play in safety because they are hidden in the
materials.
But most of the time we the people are running.
The women have skirts over-long and dragging. I have bare legs.
And we always feel a little frightened, as if someone were chasing
after us to ruin our fun. Even there.
There is no one to protect us
—not men—not laws—not fathers—or guides—no one.

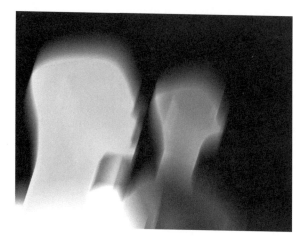

X:

Her father's television bores a hole across time.
Through it I can only see awaiting me a series of obstacles and worse.
Uniforms, shadows, tricks.
I remember that in Tis of Thee there were no guns, no bombs, no poisons.
We made it into a quiet place, rising from old waste-heaps, and the basins of sewage plants.
Just as the knuckles of trees underground can burst open the pavement, given time, so this strange little place, given patience, might also overcome.

But it was only a wish, a hope. . . .
Dogs barking under the stars, tents, fountains. . . .

Z:

Like her, he knew Scripture by heart
but was for his whole life lonely and bitter.
Intoxicated nightwalks no one knew about: his effort at transcending the day's
bright laughter.
Several times she passed him only blocks away.
Now the neutering effect of aging was reducing him—and her—to a singular
without value. He felt himself becoming more equal to others his own age, and
as they all approached invisibility, they seemed to blend,
losing the particularity guaranteed by energy.

X:

The sight of children at day's end returning to where they began, like little pris-
oners for whom jail would later become an option, finally overwhelmed me.
I saw them as orphans, uprooted, abandoned, forlorn.
For a time I drove a truck to deliver oysters in town.
It seemed like an easy situation for someone depressed and reclusive, as I was
then.
Once on my route, a woman I thought was my child's mother was standing out-
side a church.
She made no special gesture but something in her posture reminded me
of a question unanswered. But by then I had trained myself to leave, um, love,
women whom I would never see again, it was the only way to lose.
In fact I stuck both his mother and the white woman in a sentence beginning
with the word she and she can never escape it and acquire a name again.

Y:

A Sunday is always in no way new. However, on one of them
I was saying the Stations of the Cross
in a public toilet in the city of Boston. At the porcelain altar
erected for the lowest of the low,
I squatted and prayed. Outside sleet was running down a coat of concrete.
My problem? Stuck with my upside out, nervous for no reason.
Then I went out and hid in the shelter of a doorway to see the world go by.
I was thinking that Jesus was still with me as a mouth and a radiant hand
and I should calm down, but something was stirring up my instincts.

And then I saw him. The father of the baby and he was close to me.
He was hunched up
in a black coat and held a newspaper over his head, as if respectfully,
and walked so close to me I could feel his heat
and smell the melancholy in his wet coat.
And for that one moment I remembered, This life is necessary after all.

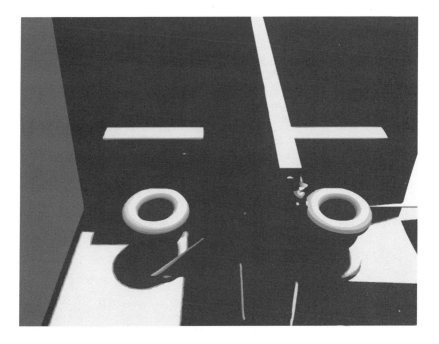

X:

I started to call out when I realized that my absence from the place
where she was actually standing
would make my voice a waste.
So I got back into my truck and drove away
into the billows of sleet. I was afraid.

Y:

He was older now and even sadder. That much was evident to me.
And like a spinster on a widow's walk, who watches the empty sea,
I felt the air and the rain between us
as a chain that would never disappear the way our poor bodies
had and would.

Z:

Yours? But what about mine? And me? Am I not of thee?

I'll answer for you, and tell you one thing I know.
Race is the most random quality assigned to a soul.
And maybe it's the very absurdity of it
that turns into obsession.

I mean, in the end it turns into something as incredible as faith.

Celebration.

A life of pure contradiction.

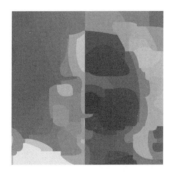

Atelos was founded in 1995 as a project of Hip's Road and is devoted to publishing, under the sign of poetry, writing that challenges the conventional definitions of poetry, since such definitions have tended to isolate poetry from intellectual life, arrest its development, and curtail its impact.

All the works published as part of the Atelos project are commissioned specifically for it, and each is involved in some way with crossing traditional genre boundaries, including for example, those that would separate theory from practice, poetry from prose, essay from drama, the visual image from the verbal, the literary from the non-literary, and so forth.

The Atelos project when complete will consist of 50 volumes.

The project directors and editors are Lyn Hejinian and Travis Ortiz. The director for text production and design is Travis Ortiz; the director for cover production and design is Ree Katrak.

Atelos (current volumes):

Distributed by:

Small Press Distribution
1341 Seventh Street
Berkeley, California
94710-1403

Atelos
P. O. Box 5814
Berkeley, California
94705-0814

to order from SPD call 510-524-1668 or toll-free 800-869-7553
fax orders to: 510-524-0852
order via e-mail: orders@spdbooks.org
order online: www.spdbooks.org

Tis of Thee
was printed in an edition of 700 copies
at Cushing-Malloy.
Illustrations and graphic design by Maceo Senna
with additional production by Travis Ortiz.
Cover design by Ree Katrak.